IN A
RUNNING BROOK

WINIFRED and CECIL LUBELL

 RAND McNALLY & COMPANY

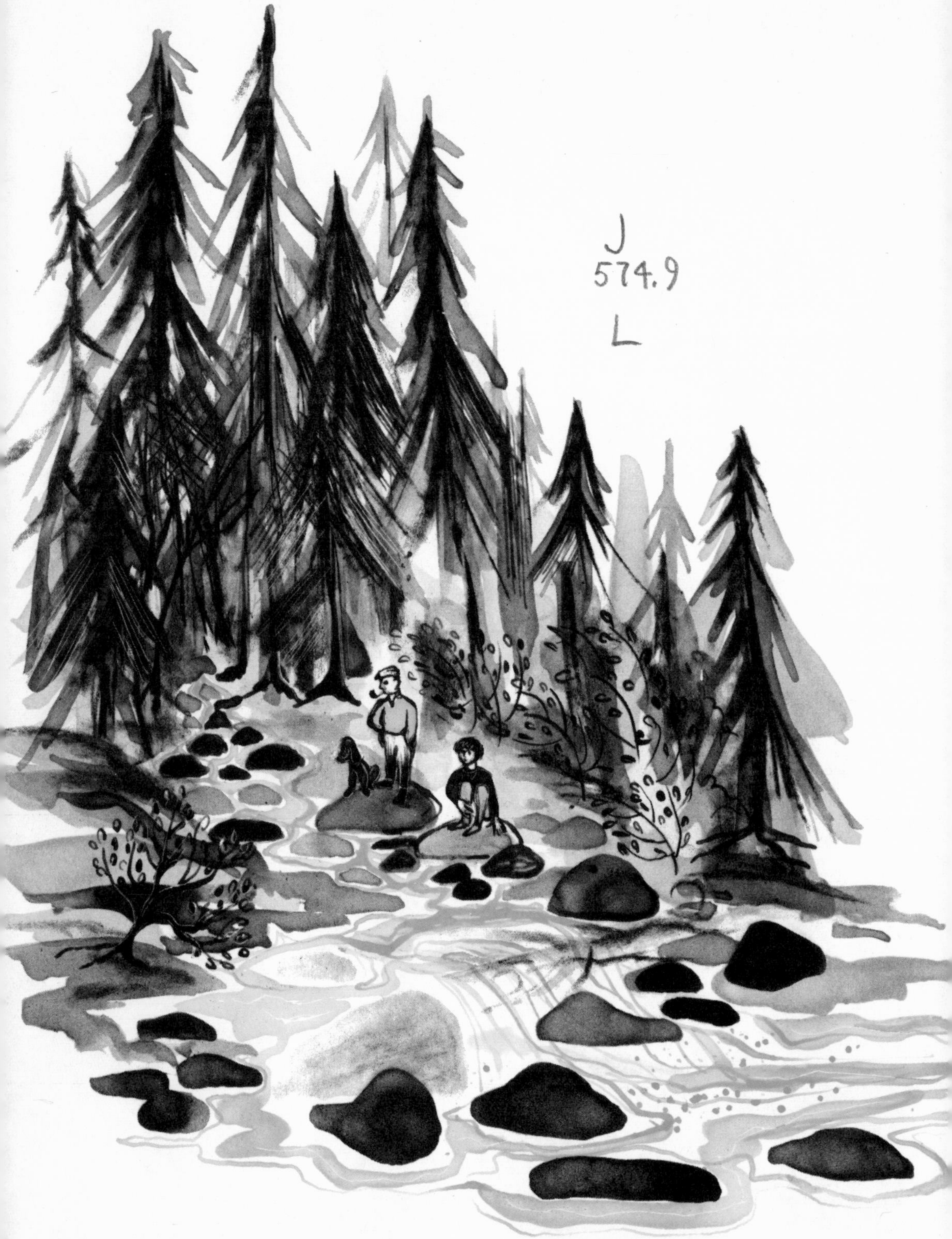

OUR BROOK

It isn't really *our* brook but we like to think of it as ours. It's a quiet, private place—so quiet and so far from the noise of streets and cars that we often feel like explorers when we go there.

To reach it we take a long path through the tall hemlock trees, walking softly on a bed of pine needles, stepping carefully over the fragile mushrooms, climbing great boulders covered with spongy moss, listening to the birdcalls and the bright chatter of the squirrels.

It's a lovely walk and at the end of the winding path runs our brook, rushing over the rocks, forming clear pools in the sunlight, and then slowing down as it snakes through the meadow beyond the woods.

This is a mountain brook. It begins high in the hills, trickling down from a spring-fed lake, and our favorite place is the mile-long course it takes through the woods before it joins the great reservoir that it helps to fill.

Often, on a sunny autumn day, we sit on the flat rocks in the middle of our brook and watch the dry leaves swirl away with the current. In spring we hear the tree frogs on the banks and see the kingfisher swoop down from the topmost branches. And once a young deer came down to drink where we sat quietly watching the darting water striders.

It's a fine place to sit and have a quiet time. But it's an exciting place, too, and we did not find this out until one hot summer afternoon when we took off our shoes and began to wade in the cool rippling water. We remember clearly how we turned over a glistening black rock under a small waterfall and found our first mayfly larva with its fanning gills . . . and then the stone-built case of a caddisworm . . . and then a tiny, flat water penny, very difficult to see with our naked eyes . . . and then the food-catching net of a different caddis.

That day the brook became a new and much more fascinating place for us, a place of many secrets to be discovered with the help of a magnifying glass.

In this book we will tell you about our discoveries.

Every brook begins with a trickle of water springing out of the ground.

Every brook gets bigger and stronger as it flows downhill from its source.

Then it is big enough to wade in, big enough for a toy boat to sail down, whipping around the rocks.

Then it is a place where deer often come to drink, a place where minnows dart and where the kingfisher dives down and snaps them from the water.

How does a brook grow? It is fed from springs, or the overflow of a pond, or the waters in a swamp. The rains help it grow, and the melting snow and ice, and the water draining from the woods and fields. In time it joins with other brooks, growing larger and deeper until it becomes a smooth-flowing stream that empties into a lake or a river and so moves down to the sea. For every brook, in time, flows down into the sea.

But there is something different about a running brook
—different from a river or a lake. There is a different kind
of animal life in its swift currents—a holdfast life. Each
of the small and sometimes tiny creatures that live in the
brook has developed a special way of holding fast to the
rocks, or of clinging to the bed of the brook, so that it
will not be washed away in the current.

In a lake the waters are usually quiet. A river generally
moves slowly on its course. But where a brook flows
downhill, the water is swift. It is always rushing, foaming,
bubbling, rippling over rocks, whirling into eddies, forming waterfalls—running, running, running. You would not
think small creatures could live in such swift waters. But
they do! They build homes, catch food, and even fasten
down their eggs against the tug of the current. And
there are many quieter spots under rushing water where
plants and rocks give these creatures safe hiding places
away from the force of the stream.

There is a strange and surprising world to be discovered
when you look closely into the running water.

STAND ON A ROCK

We stand on a rock in the middle of the brook and listen to the sound of the water. How different from the sound of the city! How different from the noise of cars and streets! A soothing sound that never begins or ends, which is always there, which fills the air, which surrounds us like the sunshine and the dark.

We stand still on the rock and look upstream. At first we see only the running water, but soon our eyes begin to pick out separate things.

There! What was that! A big green frog has been sitting on a stone quietly watching us. It was so well camouflaged that we thought it was a moss-covered rock. Then its big eyes shifted, and we moved too suddenly. That was a mistake! It took fright and jumped into the water with a clean "plop."

You can always find frogs around the brook because they are hatched from eggs laid in the water. They begin as tadpoles, breathing through gills (like fish) and living only in water. Later they grow into frogs—with lungs—and can live on land. But they still need water, or a damp place, because they take in air through their skins—as well as through their lungs—and this works only when their skins are wet. They take in water through their skins, too; not through their mouths.

And, of course, you will aways find them by the brook in springtime. Then the females lay their eggs in the water so that new tadpoles can be hatched and that's when you hear the croaking of the male frogs. It's their mating call.

A female frog can lay more than 5,000 eggs in one season. It's lucky they don't all hatch or we'd have a plague of frogs as they had in Egypt long ago.

The salamander has a sticky tongue shaped like a mushroom.

TURN OVER A STONE

We turn over a stone by the side of the brook and have our net ready. We're out to catch a salamander and they move fast!

Three inches long, or sometimes four, it's the color of straw, with two dark stripes running from its head to its long slender tail. It looks like a lizard except that it has no scales and is absolutely harmless, with a soft, moist, velvety skin that feels cool and trembling on the palm of your hand.

This one is called a Two-Lined Salamander because of its two stripes, but there are many other kinds of brook

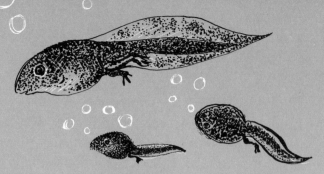

salamanders with names to fit. Perhaps in your brook you will find larger ones such as the Red Salamander, the Purple, the Dusky, or the Long-Tailed.

The Two-Lined Salamanders live beside the water and spend most of their time in the brook because they have no lungs for breathing in the air. They must all breathe through their thin skins and for that purpose their skins must always be wet, whether they are in the water or out of it—the same as frogs.

Also like frogs, their eggs are laid in water. When they hatch, they look like frog tadpoles, but you can tell them apart because they have feathery gills on each side of their necks. Later, when the salamander is full grown, the gills disappear.

You can keep them as pets. They are very shy and gentle creatures that come out of their hiding places only at night and on cloudy or rainy days. So keep them in a dark, wet place with stones and moss.

They eat insects, small worms, and tiny snails. Some of them—such as the Two-Lined Salamander—have most unusual tongues. They're shaped like mushrooms, with a stem and a big, flat cap. And the cap is very sticky, like old-fashioned flypaper or Scotch tape. When the salamander is hunting an insect, it shoots out this long, sticky tongue and down goes the insect, stuck fast to the cap.

If there should be an accident and one of your pet salamanders loses a tail—or even a leg—don't be unhappy. It will grow a new one just as your hair grows again after you cut it.

AIR IN THE WATER

The salamander and the frog can breathe under water —as well as on land. That's why scientists call them amphibians. The name comes from two Greek words: *Amphi* means "of both kinds" and *bios* means "life." They live two kinds of life—on land and under water.

They can live two lives because they have two ways of breathing.

In order to live—whether on land or in water—all creatures must have a way of taking oxygen into their bloodstreams. You and I get it through our lungs. To stay under water we must take a supply of oxygen with us by using a snorkel or an aqualung.

But most creatures living in water get oxygen from the water itself, because most water contains oxygen which it absorbs from air and from growing plants.

You and I have no way of getting oxygen from water, but fish do this through their gills. The walls and tiny blood vessels of these gills are thinner than a human hair. Tadpoles of frogs and salamanders also have gills until they are full grown, and every animal in the water has one way or another of using the oxygen that has been dissolved in the water.

The more oxygen in the water, the better it is for life. That's why there are so many living things in the brook. It's rich in oxygen absorbed by the water as it runs over rocks, turning white with bubbles of air.

CATCH A STONE FLY

This is what we do on a hot summer day . . .

We take off our shoes and step into the cool, running brook to see what we can find.

The creature we often find is a big one, so we don't need a magnifying glass. It is one or more inches long, with a flat, brown-yellow body, and four graceful feelers —two from its head and two from its tail.

It's called a stone fly because it hides under stones in tight places where its flat body will fit. There it can hold fast with strong claws against the current of the water.

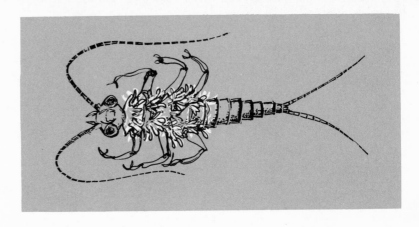

Turn a stone fly over on its back to see the white gills and strong claws. It's about an inch long, but we've drawn it much larger here.

As to the "fly" in its name . . . well, it can't fly yet, while it lives under water, but it will one day, perhaps in two or three years when it's full grown. At this stage it's a young stone fly, known as a nymph, and there are lots of them in our fast-running brook.

In fact, if a brook has no stone flies that's often a bad sign. It could mean the water is polluted. Stone flies need lots of oxygen in order to live, and polluted water usually has very little oxygen.

But if a brook has many stone flies you can be fairly sure it also has trout. Stone flies are a favorite food of trout. That's why fishermen make imitations of them as trout bait. They call them "browns."

The way we recognize a stone fly is by turning it over on its back. It looks fierce but it can't hurt us. If we look closely, we see small white tufts on its underside where the legs join the body. Those are its gills. We don't hold it more than a minute because it can't live long out of running water.

Before it's full grown a stone fly may shed its skin as many as twenty times, each time getting a better fit until the last time, when it has lost its gills and has grown four gray wings. Then it leaves the water and flies away.

A SWARM OF MAYFLIES

Late one afternoon in May, we were sitting beside a quiet part of the brook when, without warning, the surface of the water began to spatter as though hailstones were falling. The sky was clear and we saw nothing falling from the overhanging trees, yet circles were forming and widening on the water, as they do when you throw pebbles. Then, suddenly, the commotion increased. Birds began to swoop down noisily from all directions and fish were leaping out of the water, snapping at small insects rising into the air.

It was a sight never to be forgotten. We realized we had been lucky enough to find the right place and the right time for the swarming of the mayflies.

Soon the air over the brook was alive with fluttering, whirling insects. The trees along the banks were covered with their winged bodies and looked as though they had suddenly grown lacy blossoms.

We began to watch very carefully, moving closer to the water so that we could see what was happening.

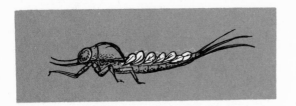

Here's the mayfly nymph, which is only about half an inch long. We've drawn it much larger than life and outlined the gills so you can see them clearly. The drawing in the circle shows how the gills look under a powerful microscope, and the one below shows how the insect looks crawling on a rock.

The brown underwater mayflies (called nymphs at this stage of their lives) were breaking through the surface of the water in great numbers and all at one time, as though they had been given a signal.

On the surface they rested a while and then—in front of our eyes—the brown skins began to split down the back and out struggled soft, gray insects, each with four delicate wings and three graceful tail feelers. With hardly a pause, they fluttered their wings and took off from the water into the air.

What a transformation! It was like the frog in the fairy tale magically changing into a prince.

We continued to watch and we saw—to our surprise— that after a short flight the newly winged insects lighted on the ground and began to split out of their skins a second time. When they emerged, they were even more beautiful than before, and as they flew off in a dancing, rhythmic flight their fragile wings glinted in the sunlight like iridescent soap bubbles.

Seen under a microscope, mayfly eggs show bumps and threads that anchor them. When the egg hatches, the insect crawls out.

This is the story of the mayfly's life. It begins—as most brook stories do—with an egg, and it ends where it began, in the brook. It begins in late spring with an egg, or rather thousands of eggs, which each female mayfly sets down in the running water.

The eggs have small bumps, or sometimes threads, and when they sink to the bottom this helps to anchor them so they won't be washed away. Still, many are swept downstream and many more get eaten. The surviving eggs hatch into mayfly nymphs.

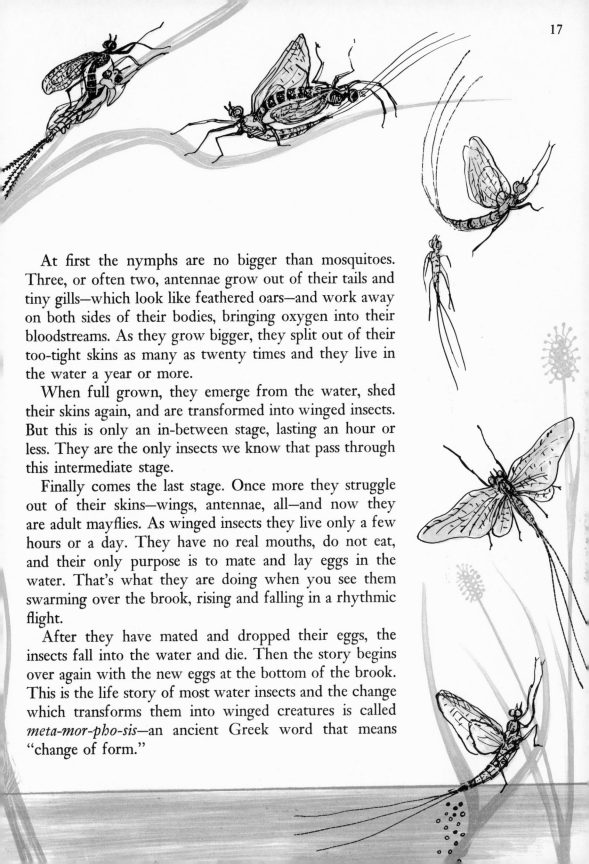

At first the nymphs are no bigger than mosquitoes. Three, or often two, antennae grow out of their tails and tiny gills—which look like feathered oars—and work away on both sides of their bodies, bringing oxygen into their bloodstreams. As they grow bigger, they split out of their too-tight skins as many as twenty times and they live in the water a year or more.

When full grown, they emerge from the water, shed their skins again, and are transformed into winged insects. But this is only an in-between stage, lasting an hour or less. They are the only insects we know that pass through this intermediate stage.

Finally comes the last stage. Once more they struggle out of their skins—wings, antennae, all—and now they are adult mayflies. As winged insects they live only a few hours or a day. They have no real mouths, do not eat, and their only purpose is to mate and lay eggs in the water. That's what they are doing when you see them swarming over the brook, rising and falling in a rhythmic flight.

After they have mated and dropped their eggs, the insects fall into the water and die. Then the story begins over again with the new eggs at the bottom of the brook. This is the life story of most water insects and the change which transforms them into winged creatures is called *meta-mor-pho-sis*—an ancient Greek word that means "change of form."

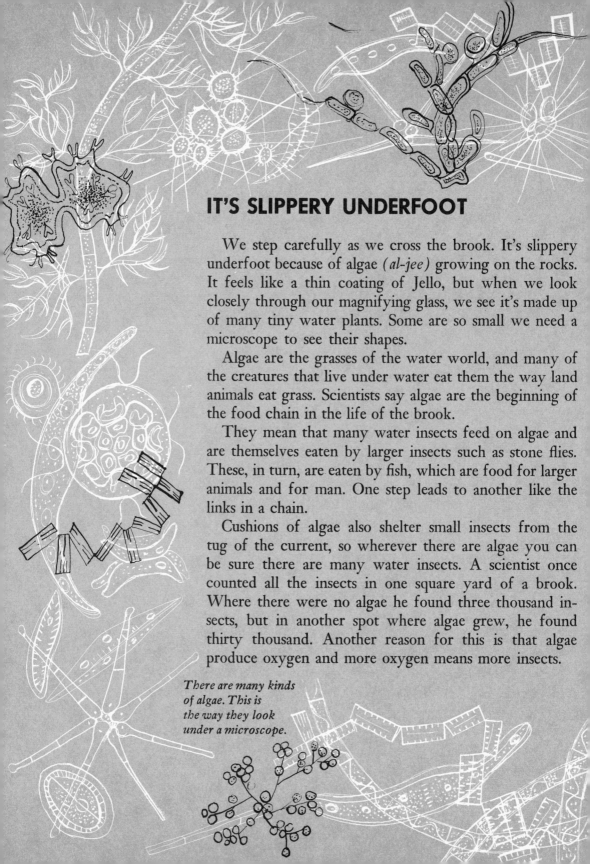

IT'S SLIPPERY UNDERFOOT

We step carefully as we cross the brook. It's slippery underfoot because of algae *(al-jee)* growing on the rocks. It feels like a thin coating of Jello, but when we look closely through our magnifying glass, we see it's made up of many tiny water plants. Some are so small we need a microscope to see their shapes.

Algae are the grasses of the water world, and many of the creatures that live under water eat them the way land animals eat grass. Scientists say algae are the beginning of the food chain in the life of the brook.

They mean that many water insects feed on algae and are themselves eaten by larger insects such as stone flies. These, in turn, are eaten by fish, which are food for larger animals and for man. One step leads to another like the links in a chain.

Cushions of algae also shelter small insects from the tug of the current, so wherever there are algae you can be sure there are many water insects. A scientist once counted all the insects in one square yard of a brook. Where there were no algae he found three thousand insects, but in another spot where algae grew, he found thirty thousand. Another reason for this is that algae produce oxygen and more oxygen means more insects.

There are many kinds of algae. This is the way they look under a microscope.

VEGETABLE OR ANIMAL?

We didn't believe it at first, but there really are sponges in the brook and they are very much like the sponges in the sea—only a good deal smaller.

They are not plants, though they look like plants. All sponges are animals, but a hundred years ago even scientists thought they were plants and many people still mistake them for some kind of moss.

That's because they don't move. They attach themselves to water-soaked logs or stones and there they stay until they die in the winter.

July and August are the best times to find them. They look like small patches of dull, yellowish fur. The patch is not just one sponge animal but a whole colony of them grown together. When we examine them under a lens we can see they are riddled with holes. These are the pores through which the water currents bring food and oxygen into the sponge and also carry out waste matter. Behind these pores the body of the animal is honeycombed with open passages. That's why sponges hold so much water.

Not all sponges are dull yellow or grow without sun. Sometimes we see bright green patches growing in the sunlight. That's because green algae have found homes inside the sponge pores.

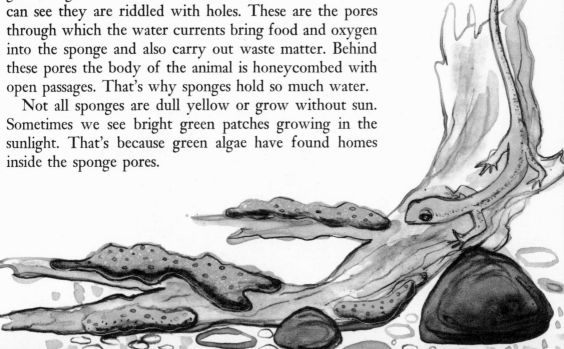

PLUMATELLA—A MOSS ANIMAL

A sponge is not the only animal in the brook that looks like a plant. There's another with the lovely name of plumatella. It's also known as a "moss animal" because it grows so much like a moss plant.

Plumatella covers underwater rocks and sunken logs with a network of fine branches the way a vine covers a wall. Like the sponge, it grows in a colony and its branches are not much thicker than a nylon fishing line. At the end of each branch is one tiny animal which resembles the cup of a flower, but is very, very small.

The first time we found plumatella covering a rock we thought it was moss. We took the rock home, set it down in a bowl of water, and began to examine it with a magnifying glass.

What a surprise we got! After a while in the water, something very strange began to happen to the little branches. Out of each flower-like cup a plume of short

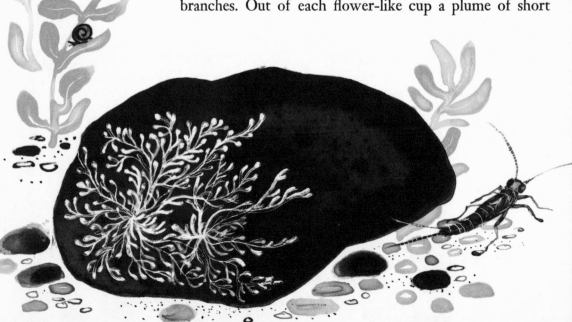

In the blue circle: plumatella, about twice life size. In the black circle: the feathery tentacles, much enlarged.

feathery tentacles suddenly emerged and began to sway back and forth like the long hair of a girl swimming under water. One second the tentacles were extended; the next, they were gone in a flash, the way a barnacle pops back into its shell.

These retractable tentacles give the animal its name. Plumatella comes from a Latin word which means "feathered," and the feathery, waving tentacles are used by the animal to search for food, which it sweeps back into its mouth in the center of the plume.

It is interesting to learn how the plumatella grows. It begins with a bud or germ formed inside the animal—a bud that looks like a tiny flattened ball ringed with a life preserver. This is called a statoblast. It is the sprout or bud that remains alive when the plumatella dies in the winter. From this bud—floating on its "life preserver"— a whole new colony of plumatella will grow in the spring.

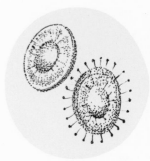

Statoblast bud from which plumatella grows. Actual size is shown at bottom left.

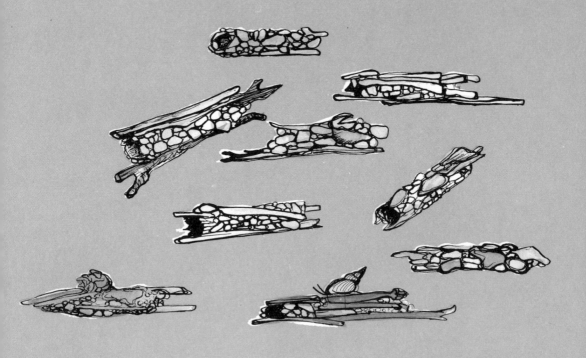

THE CASE BUILDERS

Odds and ends of bits of sticks and stones! That's what they looked like to us when we first saw them on the bed of the brook. But we were quite wrong.

They're caddis cases—protective coverings built by the caddis insect which lives under water until it is full grown and can fly. At first these cases seem to be only bits of trash, but when you examine them closely you see they have all been neatly glued together—piece to piece, stick to stick, stone to stone, and tiny stick to tiny stone.

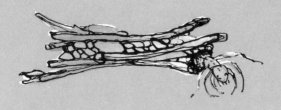

Some caddisworms make their cases from the shells of tiny snails and clams.

You find them under the rocks. They are hollow inside and they fit the caddis like a mummy case, but more loosely. The insect can crawl in and out, and water can flow through, bringing food and oxygen.

There are many types of caddis insects and they are all skillful case builders. They use many different materials, depending on what part of the brook they live in, and what building materials they find there.

Many of them have sharp mouth parts with which to cut building materials into small rectangular pieces, and all of them produce a sticky substance which they use to glue all the odds and ends of pieces together into a solid case.

Some use sticks and stones. Some use leaves and grass, bits of bark, straw, and pine needles. One type sticks together the shells of tiny snails and clams. Another makes a case out of sand grains which looks so much like a snail shell that it fools you unless you examine it with a magnifying glass. Others make cases of silk that they spin as spiders do. Some build stone corrals, often with compartments where they live together. These are the bright green caddisworms.

The case protects the caddis from other insects and also from the tug of the current in the brook. Where the

Caddis case made from sand grains. Actual size: ●

Caddis cases from a stony brook.

The little caddisworm at right looks like the creature above, when magnified.

current is strong, you find the cases weighted down with small stones. Often there are dozens of them stuck to the sides and bottoms of big rocks to keep them from being washed downstream.

Where the current is not so powerful, as in the meadow brook, the cases are usually built of lighter materials such as leaves, bits of stems, and grains of sand. Then the case is light enough so the caddis can poke the front of its body out of the tube and drag the case behind it with its strong, hooked forelegs. It makes you think of a small tractor pulling a huge log and it's a strange sight to see these bits of sticks suddenly come to life and move around jerkily on the bed of the brook.

Inside the case is an underwater insect that looks a good deal like a worm, but it's not really a worm at all. It's the larva, or early stage in the life of an insect, which later changes into a caddis fly with wings and is often mistaken for a moth.

The name larva is an interesting term because it comes from a Latin word meaning "mask." A mask is something that conceals, and in a way the winged caddis fly really *is* "concealed" in the wingless caddis larva. To emerge, it must go through metamorphosis—like the mayfly, but with an extra stage called the *pupa*. As it grows bigger, in stages, it often has to abandon the old case, which has become too small for its body, and it then constructs a new case to fit.

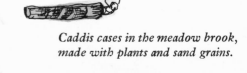

Caddis cases in the meadow brook, made with plants and sand grains.

Metamorphosis of caddis, from worm to winged insect.

At the last stage (the pupa) it closes itself in its case for about two weeks, spins a cocoon, and changes into a winged insect. Then it cuts its way out of the cocoon, swims to the surface, splits out of its pupal skin and emerges as a full-grown caddis fly.

During the larva and the pupa stages the caddis has gills so that it can breathe under water. Then, when it changes into a caddis fly, the gills are gone and it can live in the air.

But the full-grown caddis fly seldom lives more than a few days—just long enough to mate and lay its eggs on the water in a jelly-like substance from which new caddis-worms are hatched by the thousands.

So many of them, and all busy, busy, busy, gluing piece to piece, stick to stick, stone to stone, and tiny stick to tiny stone.

LOBSTERS IN THE BROOK?

We always thought that lobsters lived only in the sea. Yet in our brook we caught a creature just like a lobster —but smaller. You can find lots of them.

They're called crayfish. Two or three inches long and pale in color, they seem to be miniature sea lobsters. Like lobsters, they have big claws, long and short antennae on their heads, eyes on stalks so that they can see all around, four pairs of walking legs, and a long jointed tail with a fan-shaped end.

Crayfish look so much like lobsters that scientists believe they must have originally come from the salt seas many millions of years ago and gradually learned to live in the fresh water of the land.

To catch a crayfish, we use a net or we might get our fingers nipped by those big claws. We turn over the stones near the bank of the brook where the water is calm. As the crayfish scuttles out of its hiding place, we scoop it up in our net and pop it into a glass jar filled with water.

Have we caught a male or a female crayfish? We can tell by examining its underside. It has a number of feathery, waving fans—called swimmerets—which the crayfish uses in swimming. The male has five pairs of these. The female has only four pairs. When the female lays her eggs, she attaches them to the swimmerets—like clusters of tiny dark grapes—and there they stay until they hatch and the young crayfish are six or seven days old. Like lobsters, they have to split out of their skins as they grow bigger.

It's fun to watch a crayfish eat! We fed ours bits of bread, meat, and fish food, but we discovered worms were its favorite food. It picked up the worm in its big claws and passed it to small claws near its mouth. It has a beltline loading system for shoveling in food.

There's one important rule for keeping crayfish. They need lots of oxygen, so the water must be changed every day. (An air pump would be even better.) We didn't know this at first and our crayfish almost suffocated. We caught it just in time. Remarkable how quickly it revived in fresh water, which has more air. Otherwise it's a tough creature and can live as long as fifteen years, growing new limbs or antennae whenever it loses one in a fight.

Newborn crayfish clinging to the mother's swimmerets.

Below: the eggs look like dark grapes.

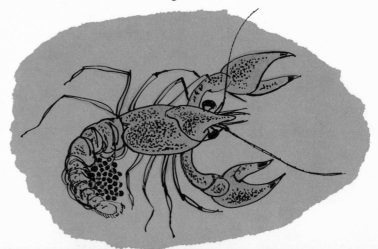

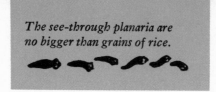

*The see-through planaria are
no bigger than grains of rice.*

SEE-THROUGH ANIMALS

In the coldest part of our brook we found tiny creatures whose ancestors lived in the glaciers during the Ice Age millions of years ago. Many of them are no larger than a grain of rice and are shaped like arrowheads with pin-dot black eyes and pointed tails. They cling to the undersides of rocks in the brook and you can pry them off gently with a penknife.

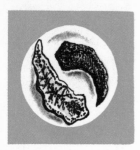

In some brooks you can collect them in a different way. Attach a string to a piece of liver and drop it into the brook. Leave it there half an hour and when you pull it up, you will sometimes find it covered with their soft bodies. They are called planaria or flatworms and they are most interesting creatures to examine with a magnifying glass.

Keep them in a jar and watch! Many of them have transparent bodies so you can see everything that goes on inside, as though you were looking through a glass insect in a museum. But here everything is alive. You can see the dark intestinal tubes branching over the whole body like a creeping vine. And sometimes you can even see the food being digested.

The planaria's mouth is not in its head but in the center of its body. When it feeds, a small tube is pushed out from the mouth and, like a suction pump, attaches itself to the food. Planaria need little food but lots of oxygen, so the water must be changed often.

Most interesting of all is the way planaria multiply. They do lay eggs, but they also divide in two. Scientists have found that when they are cut in half, each half grows a new part to replace the one cut off.

*When planaria are magnified,
you can see the inner structure
and feeding tube.*

DISCOVERIES

Brooks are full of surprises when you explore below the surface. You see little on top, but under the water millions of creatures are moving, breathing, hunting food, being born, growing, changing, dying—all hidden from sight unless you know how to look.

Our first excitement came when we turned up a bright salamander, scurrying out from under a stone. Our first surprise was to learn that the underwater nymph of a stone fly and a mayfly later grows into a winged insect. From the slippery algae we found out about the food chain in the brook. The sponge and the plumatella both surprised us by being animals, not plants.

The caddisworm was an even greater surprise, moving about in its carefully glued case. We thought at first the crayfish was a tiny lobster, transported from the sea. And the planaria, with its strange mouth, was fascinating to watch through a lens.

These were our first discoveries. Later, there were many more surprises as we began to explore the swifter waters of our brook.

HOLDFAST

Drop a leaf into the rushing current of the brook and it whirls away out of sight. Yet here, where the water is swiftest, the mosses and the liverwort find a way to grow, and many living creatures make their homes. Here we found the water penny and the net-building caddis called hydropsyche (*hy-dro-sy-key*). Here live the big-footed snail and the larvae of the blackfly and the midge. And each of these creatures has a holdfast, each has a special way of clinging tightly to rocks or plants against the pull of the swift water. Just think what it would be like if humans tried to live under the torrent of Niagara Falls. Yet to the tiny water penny, the smallest riffle in the brook is as big and powerful as Niagara is to us, and this is where it spends its early life.

A PLACE TO HIDE

To small creatures living in swift water, brook moss is a good hiding place. It grows in a carpet of tiny dark leaves or, sometimes, in long streamers (called Fountain Moss) which wave in the current. Underneath these mosses the smallest brook animals find protection from larger animals. Here they have something to cling to in the rushing water. But how does the moss itself cling against the current? At low water it puts out hairlike threads which attach themselves to rocks and to the banks. In this way the moss takes so strong a holdfast that even in springtime, when the water is a torrent, the plants are not torn loose from their anchors. Moss grows in calmer waters too and, of course, other types of moss grow in the woods. But wherever it grows, it always needs to be moist. In that way it's like the frog.

WHAT IS A LIVERWORT?

Another water plant, often mistaken for moss, has the strange name of liverwort. This simply means a liver-shaped plant. "Wort" was the old English word for root or plant, and in ancient times people believed the liverwort would cure diseases of the liver. It grows flat on the banks and on rocks rising out of the brook and it looks a little like seaweed. In fact, scientists say the liverworts did grow in the sea many millions of years ago, and that they were perhaps the first plants in the world to move onto the land.

PENNIES IN THE BROOK

One of the smallest and flattest creatures in the rapids is called a water penny. It doesn't look like a penny but it often has a coppery color and that probably accounts for its name. It is oval in shape and about the size of an apple seed.

It took us a long time to find a water penny because it's so small and because, at first, we didn't know how to search for it. The best way, we discovered, was to turn over a rock in the fast water and run our fingers along the bottom and sides until we felt a small bump. Often the bump was a water penny and its whole body was stuck to the rock so tightly that we had to pry it loose gently with a knife. Then we understood how so small a creature could manage to live in the rapids without being washed downstream.

The water penny is much smaller than the tip of your finger.

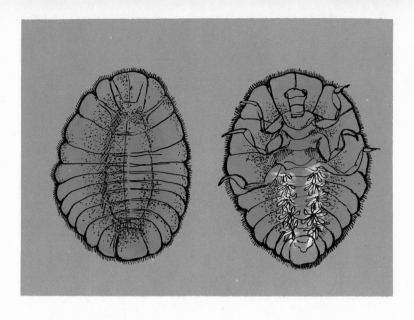

The water penny has a jointed back, which can be seen through a magnifying glass. On its underside it has six legs and white gill tufts.

Once we held the water penny in our hand we were able to examine it with a magnifying glass. The tiny bump then looked like the creature drawn here.

Its back is a jointed shell which reminds us of a lobster's tail, and all around the edge is a fringe of delicate hairs. When we turned the insect over, we found it had six tiny legs and tufts of white gills like a stone fly. As we watched it through the magnifying glass we could see it arching its jointed shell and waving its legs, trying to turn itself over. Finally it succeeded and scurried across our hand, tickling us with its tiny claws.

This water penny is the larva of a small black beetle which lives out of water all its life except when it goes back to lay its eggs in the rapids. The adult beetle has no gills and scientists asked themselves how it could breathe under water. They found that it takes its own air supply down into the water by trapping air in the hairs that cover its body.

THE NET BUILDERS

Of all the creatures in our brook, the most extra-ordinary, we think, is the hydropsyche which lives in the rapids. It's less than half an inch long and it belongs to the caddis family. Like other caddisworms (and like the spider) it can produce a silky thread. Out of this it spins a case which it later strengthens by attaching sand grains and small pebbles.

Then it does something most extraordinary. At the tip of its case it constructs a neat silken net about the size and shape of a small thimble. The mouth of the net faces upstream and is propped open with bits of twigs or pine needles. The small closed end is attached to the hydropsyche's case and there the worm waits until something is washed down by the current and caught in the net. Then, if it's hungry, the hydropsyche simply crawls out of its case and feeds on its catch, which usually consists of algae, tiny water animals, and especially blackfly larvae.

Now this, in itself, is not so unusual. A spider, for example, also spins a net to catch its food. But there's a big difference. A spider works in the open air, while a hydropsyche—and this is hard to believe—actually spins its net *under* water, in the swiftest part of the brook and right in the path of the rushing current. To realize how difficult this is, imagine a man building a house in the path of a hurricane.

The hydropsyche nets are hard to find at first because they are often woven into a patch of moss and it takes a while before your eyes get used to seeing their small and delicate shapes under the water. But when you find the first one, you begin to see many more. A scientist once counted 166 little nets on a single rock in the rapids of a brook where there also were lots of blackfly larvae for the caddis to feed on.

We ourselves were lucky enough to find one small stone with four nets and cases attached to it so that we were able to carry it home without disturbing the nets. We've made an enlarged drawing of this stone on the opposite page so you can see how skillfully the nets are constructed.

It's not easy to find the net-building caddisworms. We've drawn them actual size, the way they look in the brook.

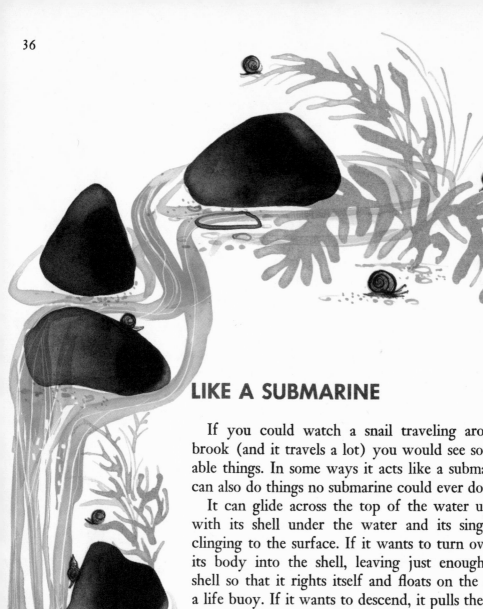

LIKE A SUBMARINE

If you could watch a snail traveling around in the brook (and it travels a lot) you would see some remarkable things. In some ways it acts like a submarine, but it can also do things no submarine could ever do.

It can glide across the top of the water upside down with its shell under the water and its single big foot clinging to the surface. If it wants to turn over, it draws its body into the shell, leaving just enough air in the shell so that it rights itself and floats on the surface like a life buoy. If it wants to descend, it pulls the foot all the way in, pushing out the air. Then it sinks to the bottom —like a submarine.

The single flat foot, which is the base of the snail's body, acts as a door or a valve, letting in or keeping out both air and water. This remarkable foot also puts out a sticky substance which lets the snail cling to the rocks as tightly as a water penny. That's why even the swiftest waterfall doesn't dislodge it.

Because of this sticky foot, snails can also glide over any surface—over rocks, up the stems of leaves and plants, along the bed and the banks. We find them in all parts of our brook, but especially in the patches of moss near the rapids and, though they are often no bigger than a pea, we can see their brown shells easily. Some are pointed and spiral, some are flat, some round and smooth, and all resemble the ocean snails to which they are related.

The body of the brook snail has two little horns or feelers, and these distinguish it from the land snail which has four feelers. There's another difference, too. The land snail has eyes at the tips of its two longer horns—like the periscope on a submarine. You would expect the same in the brook snail, but it isn't so. Its eyes are at the base of its feelers.

Some snails have two or even three sets of jaws and all snails have a ribbon-like tongue covered with horny teeth. They use it as a file to scrape off the algae and other plant matter on which they feed. That's why it's good to keep a snail or two in an aquarium. Those rough tongues scrape away the scum which makes the glass walls of the aquarium cloudy.

A FLY WITH A LIFELINE

There's a pest around our brook called a blackfly. We see swarms of them around swift-running brooks and fishermen hate them because of their nasty bite. But before this insect turns into a flying pest, it's a harmless wormlike creature—about half an inch long—which lives in the rapids and is interesting to us for at least three reasons.

First, it can spin a lifeline. We know that an astronaut is attached to his ship by a lifeline when he "takes a walk" in space. And we know that a mountain climber ties a rope around his waist and attaches it to the cliff in case he should fall. The blackfly larva—which lives in swift currents—has developed the same kind of protection. It spins a silken line and attaches it to a stone or stem. Then, if it loses its hold, the current doesn't wash it downstream. The insect pulls itself back along the lifeline—as a mountaineer does.

In black circle: blackfly larva in its case. In green area: cluster of larvae on a rock.

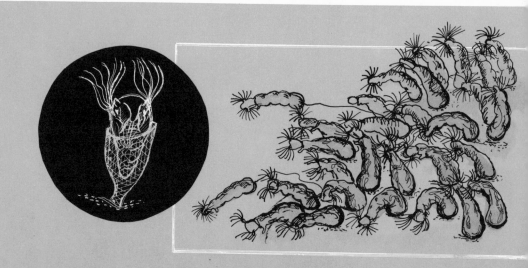

The second interesting thing about a blackfly larva is that it attaches its hind end to a rock or plant, leaving the rest of its body floating free in the fast current. It can do so because it has a sticky suction cup, with teeth, which anchors it firmly to the rock or plant. There's a good reason for this. As the head of the insect waves back and forth in the water, it collects food with two feathery fans near its mouth—very much like the plumatella. When we see a cluster of these insects living close together on a rock, they seem like a patch of dark moss waving in the current of the running water.

The third and perhaps the most fascinating thing about this insect is the way it turns from worm to fly. First it spins a silk case shaped like an ice-cream cone in which it stays under water for about two weeks. Then it splits out of its skin and from the old skin comes a tiny bubble of air which rises quickly to the surface and bursts. Out of this burst bubble comes the fly, so light that it can run on the surface of the water until it finds something to clutch. Then its wings dry in the air and it flies off to become the biting plague of fishermen, together with those other pests—gnats, midges, and mosquitoes.

IN THE QUIET POOL

Down below the rapids, where the blackfly and the hydropsyche live, our brook widens and the current flows silently into a quiet pool. A flat rock juts out into the pool and we like to sit there on a summer morning, watching the busy life around us.

The water is deep and the surface calm. Near the bank the minnows dart in rows as quick as rain. The water striders and the whirligigs skate in and out of the shadows cast by the rock. Brilliantly colored damselflies flutter in the air, which is cut by shafts of sunlight breaking through the umbrella of the trees. Shooting back and forth between the shafts, like airplanes crossing through the beams of searchlights, zoom the hunting dragonflies. Above our heads the kingfishers perch on overhanging branches, and from time to time one of them swoops down with a loud flutter of wings to snatch a minnow from the water.

Often we can see the shadowy form of a fat trout swimming noiselessly upstream against the current. The trout is a fast swimmer and lives only in fast brooks and streams where the water is cold and holds lots of oxygen. In hot weather trout stay close to the bed of the brook where the water is colder, but when they are hungry they leap out of the pool to snap at mayflies and other insects near the surface. Then we hear a sudden "plop" breaking the silence of the pool and the rings of water begin to spread where a fish has dropped back into the brook.

For us the most interesting thing about a trout is the way it lays its eggs. In autumn, the female fish chooses a shallow sandy spot in the lower part of the brook.

There she carefully digs a narrow pit with her tail while her mate hovers nearby to guard her. When the pit is finished, she sinks into it to lay her eggs and the male fish fertilizes them with sperm from his body. Then the female covers the eggs with gravel to protect them until they hatch.

It's a fascinating sight, and one day you may be lucky enough to see this happening in a brook.

MUSSELS, ALIVE, ALIVE-O

When we first began to explore our brook we had no idea we would find shellfish in the quiet pool. We thought clams and mussels lived only in the sea. But we now know a great many of them live in fresh water—in lakes, in rivers, and along the bed of our brook.

Scientists tell us life on earth began in the sea, and that many millions of years ago plants and creatures from the ocean began to move up onto the land.

It's easy to see that many of the plants and animals in our brook resemble their ancestors in the ocean. Algae are like seaweed. Brook sponge is like sea sponge. Crayfish look like miniature lobsters. Snails and fish live in both salt water and fresh water. And the same is true of mussels and clams.

The pearly black mussels and the little white-shelled clams in our brook are hard to tell apart from those in

the ocean. They live in the mud and sand on the brook bed, and the way some of them grow is one of the most interesting stories in nature.

In spring, female clams and mussels form their eggs inside their shells. With some types, the eggs hatch and grow inside the shell until they are big enough to care for themselves. But with many other types (and only in fresh water) a remarkable event takes place.

The eggs—many thousands of them—hatch inside the mother's shell and become tiny shellfish no bigger than a pinhead. These are called glochidia (*glow-kid-e-uh*), and each one has a sharp point at the end of its shells which it can snap open and shut like pincers.

Shown here very much enlarged is a young mussel with snapping shell, ready to clamp onto passing fish.

If these tiny glochidia were allowed to fall free into the water, most of them would smother and die in the mud. To prevent this, the mother mussel and clam wait for a passing fish and then shoot a stream of glochidia up at the fish. As the glochidia surround the fish, their sharp pointed shells are snapping open and shut, trying to attach themselves to the gills and fins of the fish. Many of them don't succeed, and they do indeed sink into the mud and die.

But many of them *do* manage to attach themselves to the fish and are saved. They live under the skin of the fish for several weeks until they are big enough to break away and survive on their own in the water.

This does not seem to harm the fish. In fact, they may even get some benefit from the glochidia, for hundreds of these tiny mussels and clams have been found on the body of a single healthy fish. Some people call them "fish blackheads."

WHO LIKES MOSQUITOES?

We don't, for sure! On muggy days around our brook the mosquitoes are so fierce they can really drive us away, even though we protect ourselves with insect repellent. Many times we've had to run for it, to escape their stings.

But to birds and dragonflies the mosquito is food on the wing. And before it grows wings, when it's still a wormlike creature under the water, the mosquito is food for fish and the nymphs of many larger insects in the brook.

So—fortunately for humans—some creatures *do* like mosquitoes and that helps keep down the mosquito population in the world.

The bite you get is a sting and only the female mosquito stings, never the male. It pricks you with a tiny hollow needle like a hypodermic and it sucks out blood which it seems to need in order to lay eggs.

Mosquitoes breed so fast they can grow in any kind of water, even in a rain puddle. In damp hot weather it takes as little as ten days for the eggs to become larvae, then pupae, then winged insects. That's why there are so many of them—often a new batch every two weeks.

The eggs are laid together in a group which forms a raft no more than a quarter-inch long, floating on the water. They hatch in a day and out come wormlike larvae called wrigglers because of the way they move.

The wriggler floats upside down just under the surface. At the tail end of its body it has a breathing tube and it pokes this tube up through the surface of the water like a periscope, while its head and the rest of its body hang suspended in the water, searching for food. Later, when it becomes a pupa, it has two breathing tubes which it pokes out above the waterline.

That's why people got the idea of spreading oil or kerosene on the surface of a pool. This kills the mosquito wrigglers and the pupae because they are not able to break through the oil slick with their breathing tubes, and so they suffocate.

Four stages in the life of a mosquito: first, a raft of eggs; second, a wriggler hanging head down; third, a pupa with two tubes above water; fourth, the winged insect emerging from the water.

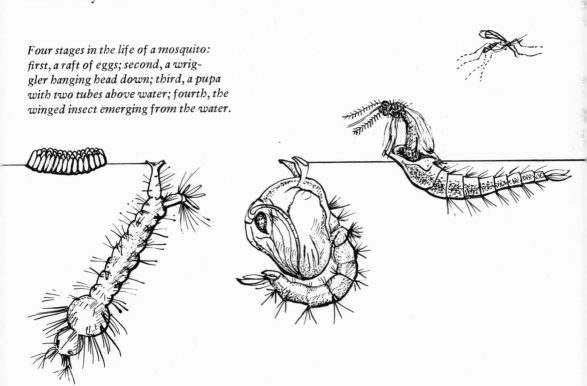

THEY SKATE ON WATER

Our favorite among all the moving creatures in our brook is an insect called a water strider, which can stand or move on top of the water without sinking in. We love to watch them darting over the surface as quick as a wink, looking like tiny racing boats with long sweeping oars.

And they're easy to find. Often, when we sit on the big rock at the edge of our brook, we see hundreds of them shooting from shadow to sunlight on the smooth surface of the pool.

As we watch them, a very interesting thing happens whenever they dart into the sunlight. They cast a strange shadow on the sandy bottom of the pool. The shadow shows the boat-shaped body of the strider, its four long and two short wiry legs, and something else which was a great puzzle to us at first. At the end of each leg we can see an oval shadow almost as large as the strider's body, and around each oval shadow is a ring of bright light.

We couldn't understand this until we tried an experiment at home. We filled a white bowl with water and set it down under a strong electric light bulb. Then we held up a spoon between the light and the water. Of course, the spoon cast a shadow on the bottom of the bowl, but there was no bright ring to be seen around the shadow. Slowly, we brought the spoon down onto the surface of the water and let it sink a little but without spilling any water over its sides. And suddenly there it was—a bright ring shining around the shadow of the spoon on the bottom of the bowl.

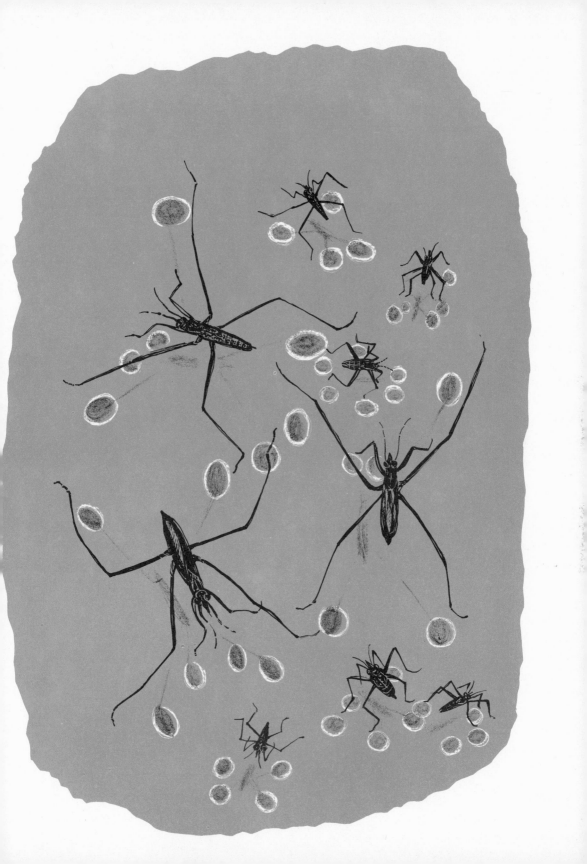

The reason for this, we discovered, is that all water has a sort of "skin" on its surface, and you can press a dimple into this "skin" without breaking through. You must do this carefully with a smooth object like a spoon or with something waxy which won't soak up the water. Then the sunlight or an electric light will form a bright ring as

it passes around the curve of the dimple in the water.

That's what happens to the water strider's shadow. Its feet are covered with waxy hairs and as they press the water they form dimples on the surface without breaking through, because the insect's body has so little weight. These dimples cast bright-ringed shadows on the sandy bottom of the pool, but the body of the strider—which is higher and doesn't touch the water—casts an ordinary shadow without a bright ring.

Sometimes, instead of six-ringed shadows, we see only four or three. That's when the strider has lifted its two front legs out of the water to grab its prey, or is cleaning itself and is standing on three legs. Then we see it suddenly dart forward by sweeping its two middle legs back like oars while it steers with its two hind legs. But unlike oars, the strider's legs move in a flash and they leave no trail in the water because they never break the surface. They skate over the top as though it were ice and that's why they are often called water skaters.

THE WHIRLING BEETLES

Often, near the water striders, we come across a whole swarm of whirligig beetles, zooming and whirling around on top of the water like tiny steel blue cars on an electric bumping ring at a fair. But they never bump. Their eyes are half in and half out of the water and they can see both above and below at the same time. Perhaps that's why they are so hard to catch. If they sense danger, they dive quickly out of sight, carrying with them a bubble of air for breathing.

THE BROOK SLOWS DOWN

Beyond the deep pool in the cool woods our brook
slows down as it widens its banks and meanders gently
through a flat, open meadowland. From the cathedral of
overhanging branches we walk downstream and step out
under the open sky. Here the brook is a different place
with a different kind of life in its waters. It is now more
like a small pond.

In the swift waters of the upper brook there are only
a few plants which can find a holdfast against the pull of
the current. But in the meadow brook the current is so
slow you can hardly see it move. Here many different
plants root and grow in the mud and sand under the
shallow water.

It is the same with the animal life. In the rapids the creatures we found had to have special ways of clinging to the rocks, of catching their food, and of fastening down their eggs so they would not be swept downstream. But in the slow-moving meadow brook we find other kinds of creatures which need no holdfast.

Like the animals that live in ponds, they can burrow in the mud and silt which has been carried downstream by the fast water and left there to settle on the shallow bed of the brook.

The meadow brook is home to the black water snake and the turtle, to the sunfish, to worms and snails of many kinds, to the diving beetle, to the back swimmer, and to the caddis which builds a case out of leaves.

It is a place of flowering plants growing in the sunlight. Plants produce oxygen as they grow. The more plants, the more oxygen in the water; the more oxygen, the more animals that can live there, for they must have oxygen to breathe. The plants also are food and shelter for underwater creatures. Between the leaves and around the stalks they find refuge from their enemies and a safe place to lay their eggs. The meadow brook is a teeming place, full of living things.

Some of the plants that grow here are quite different from those on land. Since their stems are supported by water, they are not stiff, but soft and pliable so they can bend in the current without breaking. And some, like the crowfoot, have two kinds of leaves—broad ones above water and ribbon-like ones under water so as not to resist the current.

In spring the edges of the meadow brook are covered with bright green skunk cabbage, broad-bladed rushes, and pale blue forget-me-nots. In July the creamy, butter-cup-shaped flowers of the water crowfoot burst into a mass of blooms. And in late August there are lovely ranks of purple loosestrife standing tall among the yellow goldenrod.

All summer the dragonflies and damselflies brighten the air with the glint of their brilliant bodies, and the spiders are everywhere, spinning their silken webs from plant to plant, sometimes even building long silken bridges across the width of the brook.

Upstream the water foams and bubbles noisily over the rocks, but here in the meadow brook the sound is soothing soft and far away.

DRAGONS AND DAMSELS

Dragons and damsels belong in ancient folk tales, not in a running brook. But the dragonflies and the damsel-flies around our brook got their names long, long ago when people told those ancient tales and believed them. They are good names, too, because they help us recognize the difference between these two insects which look so much alike.

The dragonfly is indeed a fierce and terrifying "dragon" to the mosquitoes it hunts. It darts in on its prey like a hawk. The damselfly is truly more damsel-like, more delicate in form, often prettier in color, and instead of zooming like a hawk, it flutters like a butterfly along the edges of the brook.

There's another difference more easily noticed. At rest, the dragonfly holds its wings out straight like an airplane while the damselfly holds its wings folded over its long slender body.

Both of these four-winged flies are the terror of mos-quitoes, gnats, midges, and other insects that are pests to people. They gobble up the pests by the thousands and we should be grateful to them for this service. In half an hour a dragonfly can eat its own weight in mosquitoes.

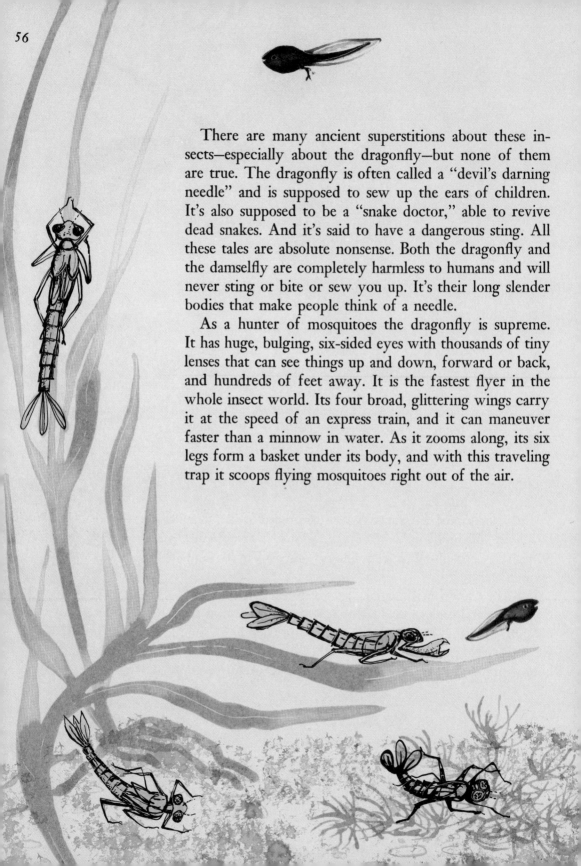

There are many ancient superstitions about these insects—especially about the dragonfly—but none of them are true. The dragonfly is often called a "devil's darning needle" and is supposed to sew up the ears of children. It's also supposed to be a "snake doctor," able to revive dead snakes. And it's said to have a dangerous sting. All these tales are absolute nonsense. Both the dragonfly and the damselfly are completely harmless to humans and will never sting or bite or sew you up. It's their long slender bodies that make people think of a needle.

As a hunter of mosquitoes the dragonfly is supreme. It has huge, bulging, six-sided eyes with thousands of tiny lenses that can see things up and down, forward or back, and hundreds of feet away. It is the fastest flyer in the whole insect world. Its four broad, glittering wings carry it at the speed of an express train, and it can maneuver faster than a minnow in water. As it zooms along, its six legs form a basket under its body, and with this traveling trap it scoops flying mosquitoes right out of the air.

Both the dragonfly and the damselfly are hatched from eggs which the female insects have dropped into the water. The young flies live under water as nymphs for as long as a year. They molt many times and are finally transformed into brilliantly colored winged insects. During the underwater stage of their lives it's very easy to tell them apart. The dragonfly is usually short and squat with a tapering body. The damselfly has a long slender body, a lot like its winged shape, with gills that resemble tail feathers. Under water both insects are just as powerful hunters as they are in the air, and one of their chief preys is the mosquito wriggler—which gives us a double reason to be grateful to them.

The way they hunt is fascinating to watch and we were able to do this by keeping a few of them in a glass jar of meadow brook water which was full of living things. They move slowly on their legs until suddenly—zip!— they dart forward, propelled by a powerful jet of water from the ends of their bodies. And something else quite remarkable happens. After they have come close to their prey, an armed and double-hinged underlip shoots far out from under their heads and grabs the prey with sharp claws. Then the lip folds back, ready for the next attack. It always reminds us of a frog's tongue flicking out to snap up a fly.

WINTER WATERS

On a cold, sun-bright day in mid-January we paid a visit to our brook.

The air was clear and sharp. The woods were covered with clean, white snow. The sky was cloudless blue and the sun shone brilliantly, casting shadow patterns of the trees on the unbroken snow.

In the brook the water was high and running fast. And it was very cold, so cold it burned our fingers when we dipped them into the rushing current.

For a while we stood quietly on a big rock rising out of the swirling water and we peered down intently to see what living things we could discover.

There were not many—or so it seemed.

By holding a kitchen sieve under an icy riffle we did find a few specimens—two small mayfly nymphs and a little brown snail—but nothing else. It was not like the brook we knew in summertime, filled with living creatures. It seemed almost empty of life, waiting for spring.

But we thought perhaps we had not been sharp enough because of the cold, so we scooped up a jarful of mud and water from the bed of the brook and carried it home to examine more carefully.

In the warm house we emptied the jar into an open dish, allowed the mud to settle, and then began to look at it through a strong magnifying glass.

We were amazed at what we saw!

Seen through a lens, the muddy water was teeming with life. It was swarming with tiny living creatures—whirling around, twisting, poking, pushing, darting from side to side, scurrying after food, fanning their gills, living, eating, fighting . . . all in that small dish of winter brook water.

For us this was a most exciting experience, and each day for a week we examined the water dish with our lens to see what new creatures we could find.

The first day there were many. We found the larvae of blackflies, mayflies, and stone flies. We found a number of planaria and five tiny snails. There was a great deal of alga, and among the algae we found the pale green nymph of a damselfly.

The second day, too, was full of discoveries, including the discarded skins of two mayfly larvae which had molted overnight. But by the third day the numbers grew fewer and by the sixth day there was very little stirring in the water except the snails.

For good reasons, too.

First, the larger creatures were eating the smaller ones and, by the sixth day, the food supply in the water dish was almost exhausted.

Secondly, our dish of brook water was rapidly losing its oxygen. It had been used up by all those creatures breathing in the water and no new supply was being added—the way it is added in the brook when the water foams over the rocks.

It seems odd to say it, but many of the animals in the dish were being "drowned" in airless water.

And so we learned that the brook is not at all dead in winter. It is filled with living creatures, just as it is in spring and summer, but they are harder to find. They are down on the bed of the brook, hidden under mud and stones, waiting for the springtime when they will rise and multiply.

HOW TO LOOK

Most of the animals that live in a brook are very, very small so that no matter how sharp your eyes are, you will need a good magnifying glass to lead you into this hidden world. When you pick up a small rock from the bed of the brook and turn it over, there seems to be nothing on it but a few glistening, watery bumps. But when you look at it through a magnifying glass, one of those bumps may turn out to be a mayfly larva with fluttering gills; and a lump of rolled-up leaves may be the case of a caddisworm. By using a glass you will see things three or more times their actual size and everything will come alive for you, as it does for us when we go exploring in our brook.

You can buy a good magnifying glass for less than a dollar in most variety stores, but it may take you a little while before you learn to use it properly. The main thing to remember is this: *hold the glass close to your eye* and then bring the object up slowly, nearer and nearer until it comes into sharp focus. You can practice by examining the skin on your thumb.

HOW TO COLLECT

For collecting you need—first of all—a running brook

and an inquiring eye. Now tie a string to your magnifying

glass and hang it around your neck so it will be handy and

leave your hands free. Next, take off your shoes and socks

and step into the water. Some people wear old

sneakers, which makes it easier to wade. If the water is very cold,

rubber boots are nice to have. A small pail or a

tinfoil pie plate are helpful for examining your catch, and

you will need one or two clear plastic pill boxes or a water-

tight jelly jar to hold your specimens. Sometimes we stuff

a couple of plastic bags into our pockets. They hold water

and you can tie the top. It's good to have a net but a

kitchen strainer will do and it's fine for scooping mud from

the brook. And sometimes it's nice to just sit on a rock in the sun and

listen to the sound of the brook without collecting anything.

INDEX

Printed in U.S.A.